Cool Cards

Creating Fun and Fascinating Collections!

Anders Hanson

ABDO
Publishing Company

Visit us at
www.abdopublishing.com

Published by ABDO Publishing Company, 4940 Viking Drive, Edina, Minnesota 55435.

Printed in the United States.

Design and Production: Mighty Media, Inc.
Cover Photos: Anders Hanson
Interior Photos: Anders Hanson; © 2006 NFL Properties LLC. Team names/logos are trademarks of
the teams indicated. All other NFL-related trademarks are trademarks of the National Football
League; Beckett Football magazine © Beckett Media LP; © 2006 NBA Entertainment; © 2006 WNBA
Enterprises, LLC; Cincinnati Redstockings card courtesy of The Cincinnati Reds; Scrye book used with
permission from Krause Publications, publisher of Scrye: *Collectible Card Game Checklist & Price
Guide*, by John Jackson Miller, Joyce Green Greenholdt & Jason Winter, 800-258-0929,
www.krausebooks.com; © 2006 The Topps Company, Inc.; © The Upper Deck Company; © Donruss
Playoff LP; Library of Congress, Prints and Photographs Division, [13163-32, no.4] and [13163-06, no. 2];
Magic: The Gathering images used with permission of Wizards of the Coast, Inc.
Series Editor: Pam Price

Library of Congress Cataloging-in-Publication Data

Hanson, Anders, 1980-
    Cool cards / Anders Hanson.
       p. cm. -- (Cool collections)
    Includes index.
    ISBN-13: 978-1-59679-773-4
    ISBN-10: 1-59679-773-8
    1. Sports cards--Collectors and collecting. I. Title. II. Series: Cool collections (Edina, Minn.)

    GV568.5.H36 2007
    796.075--dc22   2006011551

Contents

It's In the Cards!

UNLIKE ROCK OR SHELL COLLECTING, CARD COLLECTING CHANGES WITH THE TIMES.
Twenty years ago, hobby shops carried mostly baseball cards as well as a few basketball, football, and hockey cards. Since then, professional athlete strikes, collectable card games (CCGs), and advances in card printing technology have changed the focus of card collecting.

Today, sports cards are printed with better inks on thicker paper stock. Rare insert cards are all the rage. But the biggest thing to happen to card collecting was CCGs, such as Magic: The Gathering and Pokémon. These games added a new dimension, head-to-head game play, to collectible cards.

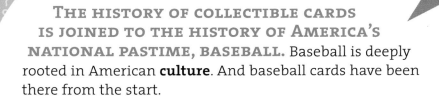

THE HISTORY OF COLLECTIBLE CARDS IS JOINED TO THE HISTORY OF AMERICA'S NATIONAL PASTIME, BASEBALL. Baseball is deeply rooted in American **culture**. And baseball cards have been there from the start.

Play Ball!

A photograph of the first professional baseball team, the 1869 Cincinnati Red Stockings, was printed on a small card. People viewed the team photograph through a magnifying glass attached to the card. Store owners in Cincinnati, Ohio, printed advertisements on the backs of these "cabinet" cards and gave them to their customers.

The First Baseball Card?

Peck & Snyder distributed the 1869 Cincinnati Red Stockings card. It is often considered the first baseball card. Its value in 2005 was about $35,000.

Sports cards caught on gradually. Around 1886, tobacco companies began to put baseball cards in cigarette packs. As baseball gained popularity in the 1930s, candy makers, such as Goudy Gum, became the main producers of baseball cards. But **World War II** soon demanded the country's attention and resources. This led to a decrease in card production.

After World War II, Americans had more free time for sports and hobbies. Two candy makers, Bowman and Topps, began putting baseball cards in packs of gum. However, by this time baseball fans were more interested in the cards than the gum.

Competition between Bowman and Topps led to improved card quality. The companies made the cards larger. They added player **statistics** to the back of each card. And, they replaced paintings and hand-colored photographs with color photographs.

JAMES RYAN.
CENTRE FIELDER - CHICAGO.

No Smoking!

Even in the early 1900s, some people were aware of the dangers of smoking. In 1909, Pittsburgh Pirates shortstop Honus Wagner demanded that all his cards be removed from cigarette packs. Wagner said he wanted his young fans to know he did not approve of smoking.

During that time, other sports caught on with American fans. Football, basketball, and hockey gained popularity. Sports collectors started to collect those cards as well as baseball cards. In 1956, Topps bought out its competitor, Bowman. It became the only producer of baseball cards until 1980.

The early 1990s saw a big boom in collectible sports cards. In 1988, Topps made the only nationally distributed set of football cards. But by 1992, there were 20 sets available from various manufacturers.

Then, the sport that started it all threatened to end it all. The 1994 baseball season was called off because the players wanted more money. Many fans thought the owners and the players cared more about money than the game itself. Thousands of people lost interest in baseball and in card collecting.

Card companies needed a way to create new interest in cards. So, they came up with the insert. An insert is a special, rare card that is more valuable than normal cards in a set. These inserts often contain pieces of jerseys, bats, gloves, or other equipment that the players used. If the item was involved in a milestone moment, the card could be worth thousands of dollars right out of the package!

Chew on This!

Topps originally used collectible cards to get people to buy its gum and candy. But in 1991, the company decided to stop putting unsealed gum in the card packs. Collectors had become concerned about card quality. They would no longer tolerate gum stains on the cards!

The New Card on the Block

In 1993, a company called Wizards of the Coast introduced a fantasy-based card game called Magic: The Gathering. Magic cards featured fierce warriors, mystical wizards, and fanciful monsters.

Instead of sports **statistics**, numbers on the cards indicated strengths and weaknesses of characters in battle. Players bought packs of cards with varying classes, skills, and strengths. They **strategically** organized their cards into "battle" decks to pit against another player's cards. Magic became a hit almost overnight, and the collectible card game was born.

Magic: The Gathering

Is It a CCG?

It might be a collectible card game if:

- The cards have characters, items, or spells with certain instructions and properties.

- First-time players can get started quickly by purchasing a starter deck.

- Players form strategic decks and compete against one another.

- It is nearly impossible to get a complete set because certain powerful cards are rare. If bought individually, they may cost hundreds or thousands of dollars.

But it wasn't until Pokémon arrived in America from Japan in 1999 that a CCG captured the entire nation's attention. The Pokémon CCG was promoted by the Pokémon television show and video games. They helped bring the characters on the cards to life through **animation** and storytelling. Pokémon's creators even gave the television show the tagline "Gotta Catch 'Em All!" This referred to the desire of card collectors to collect all the Pokémon cards.

But a few years later, another hot CCG called Yu-Gi-Oh! swept Japan off its feet. And it too was **poised** to capture the American audience.

Like Pokémon, Yu-Gi-Oh! had its roots in Japanese animation. It too was supported by television programs and video games. But, its darker plots and **intriguing** characters appealed to a broader audience than Pokémon's cute pocket monsters. By 2002, Yu-Gi-Oh! had eclipsed Pokémon. It was living up to the meaning of its name, "The King of Games."

The success of Yu-Gi-Oh! and Pokémon triggered a wave of new CCGs like X-Men, Pirates of the Caribbean, and Star Wars.

X-Men

Elements
of a Sports Card

The Front

Player portrait

The photo or drawing of the athlete

Player name

The athlete's name or nickname

Player number

The number on the player's jersey

Team logo

The official logo of the athlete's team

Manufacturer

The company that produced the card

Team name

The name of the athlete's team

Player position

The position the athlete plays

Card brand

The brand name of this card

These diagrams are guides to the types of information that are included on a sports card. Every card is a little bit different. Not all cards have the same types of information.

The Back

Card number
The card's number within the set

Production year
The year the card was produced

Player data
Brief physical information

Statistics
Game statistics from previous years

Education
The school the player last attended

Biography
History or career highlights

League logo
The official logo of the sports league

Protective mark
A mark that discourages forgery

Sports Cards

MAYBE YOU'RE INTERESTED IN GETTING SOME HOT INSERT CARDS. Or, maybe you just like the excitement of a surprise. Either way, opening a fresh pack of sports cards can be really fun! But, if you have a specific goal, such as owning your favorite player's card, you'll probably want to buy it individually or trade for it.

Opening a pack of cards is fun because you never know what you'll find inside. Not all unopened packs are cheap, though. Packs that are guaranteed to have a certain number of inserts or packs of special subset cards may cost much more. Some packs today can cost up to $100!

Some people actually save the unopened pack as a collector's item. Older unopened packs can become valuable if they contain a **coveted** card, such as the **rookie** card of a current Hall of Famer.

Old Gold

In 1969, an unopened pack of Topps baseball cards sold for ten cents. In 2005, the same unopened pack was worth about $900! That's an increase of 899,900 percent!

Types of Cards

Basic cards

Basic cards are the core of sports card collecting. They generally include every player from a league, and often more. They are reasonably priced, but they are not as desireable as parallel or insert cards.

Parallel cards

Parallel cards look similar to basic cards, but the card design has been noticeably altered. Often, this is achieved by changing the border or background color of a card. Parallel cards are scarcer than basic cards. That makes them harder to collect, as well as more valuable.

Insert cards

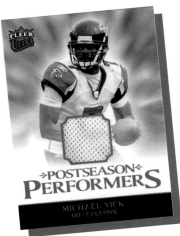

Inserts are the hot trend in sports card collecting today. It can be thrilling to find an **autographed** card or a piece of a famous player's jersey inside a pack of **random** cards. Inserts are rare and can sometimes be worth a good deal of money. Types of inserts include autographs, pieces of historic game-used bats, and scraps of player-worn jerseys, gloves, and hats. Insert cards may also feature special printing or **etching**.

Other Types of Cards

ROOKIE CARDS

A **rookie** card is the first card issued by a major card company for an athlete. It takes time to make the cards, so they don't always come out during a player's first year in the major leagues. Rookie cards are often rare, and that increases their value. Rookie cards are almost always worth more than basic cards issued later in an athlete's career. Having a rookie card is like holding a piece of that player's history.

ERROR CARDS

Occasionally a manufacturer makes a mistake when printing or producing a card. If it is a bad error on a popular player's card, the error could increase the card's value. But more often than not, errors decrease or have little effect on the price of a card.

Types of Collections

TEAM COLLECTIONS

If you have a favorite sports team, it might be fun to try to collect all its players' cards from a certain year. If the team plays in your hometown, it should be easy to find most of the cards. If your team plays well that year, the value of its set could increase notably.

PLAYER COLLECTIONS

Sports fans usually have at least one favorite athlete who inspires them. For most collectors, it's only natural to set aside their favorite player's cards so they can admire and show them off more easily. Usually, a player's most desired cards are **rookie** cards or rare inserts.

COMPLETE SETS

Today there are many different types of sets. These include base sets, parallel sets, and inserts. It's a real challenge to collect complete sets. But, it can be very satisfying when you find the card that completes a set.

Elements of a Collectible Card

Card number

The card's number within the set

Artwork/Photo

An image of the card's featured character

Card effects

How the card affects game play

Attack/Defense

Values that determine how powerful the card is

Card title

The name of the card's item, character, or spell

Artists

The illustrators or photographers who created the artwork

Edition

The edition number for this set of cards

Protective mark

A mark that discourages forgery

This diagram is a guide to the types of information found on a collectible card. Every card is a little bit different. Not all cards have the same types of information.

Collectible Card Games

© Wizards of the Coast, Inc.
Image used with permission.

THERE ARE MORE THAN 150 DIFFERENT KINDS OF COLLECTIBLE CARD GAMES. That can make it difficult to decide which ones to collect. Most collectors start with a game that their friends already collect. Then, they can battle it out with other players in head-to-head competition. That's what makes CCGs so fun!

Cool CCGs

In 2006, some of the most popular CCGs were:

- Yu-Gi-Oh!
- Magic: The Gathering
- Pokémon
- Pirates of the Caribbean
- Star Wars
- X-Men

STARTER DECKS

Many CCGs have starter decks, which include all the cards and accessories you need to get started. Starter decks are a great way to begin playing a new CCG. Most are fairly inexpensive. And, they give collectors a solid base to build on.

Popular CCGs, such as Yu-Gi-Oh!, release new starter decks a couple times a year. Cards in starter decks are not **random**, but they do vary from season to season. Later, you can improve a starter deck with cards you find in random packs or with cards you purchase individually.

Yu-Gi-Oh!

Yu-Gi-Oh! began as a Japanese comic. Its characters play a card game called Duel Monsters. Duel Monsters mirrors the real-life CCG played by millions of Yu-Gi-Oh! collectors. To play Yu-Gi-Oh!, a collector constructs a deck of Monster, Magic, and Trap cards to battle against another player's deck.

THEMED DECKS

Themed decks are like starter decks, but they appeal to more experienced players. These players have multiple decks for different situations. Themed decks are usually specific sets of cards that work well together. For example, some CCG companies release themed decks that mirror the winning decks from large tournaments.

BOOSTER PACKS

Most CCG collectors build their decks by buying unopened packs called booster packs. Nearly all CCGs have rare and powerful cards that can be found only in booster packs or bought individually for a high price. It can be really exciting to find rare cards in fresh packs. Of course, you're much more likely to find common cards that aren't as powerful. But you never know for sure, and that's part of the fun!

© Wizards of the Coast, Inc. Image used with permission.

Magic: The Gathering

Magic: The Gathering was the first collectible card game. It was introduced in 1993. By 2006, it had attracted about 6 million players worldwide! The game has a fantasy theme. Its characters, items, and spells are similar to those found in Dungeons & Dragons or the Lord of the Rings trilogy.

Pokémon

The Pokémon CCG is based on Japanese **animation.** The creator of the Pokémon series, Satoshi Tajiri, liked to collect insects as a child. When Tajiri combined his love of collecting insects with CCGs, he came up with the basic concept of Pokémon. As well as being the name of the game, the word *Pokémon* also refers to the characters, or "pocket monsters," within the game.

INDIVIDUAL CARDS

If you have a **strategy** in mind that requires one or more specific cards, you may want to buy them individually. It won't be as exciting as finding the cards in a pack. But, you'll be sure to get what you're looking for.

Unfortunately, buying cards individually can be expensive. Certain rare CCG cards have sold for several thousand dollars! But don't let that scare you. Almost all CCG cards can be purchased for less than $20. Most CCG cards cost less than a dollar.

Game Play

Each CCG has different strategies and rules. But, each game does require a strategically built deck. To form this deck, each player chooses about 40 cards from his or her collection. During the game, players **randomly** select cards from their decks to pit against cards from another player's deck. Each card has a description of its abilities in battle or its effects on other cards.

Research and Resources

How Much Is a Card Worth?

Card collectors love to know how much their cards are worth. The value of a card changes constantly. Value is affected by how many copies of the card are available and how many people want to own one.

The three best resources to find the value of a card are online price guides, magazines, and books. Some serious collectors check all of these resources. This is because prices vary from one publication to another. However, most people find that one price guide is plenty.

Online price guides

If you have access to the Internet, online price guides are a great option. The best thing about online price guides is that they're interactive. You don't have to search through a whole magazine or a book for a card's value. Instead, you type in the player or character's name, the year of the card, or the company that produced it. The search results will display the value of any cards that match your search.

Of course, not every online price guide is the same. There are a few free online price guides, such as those at collect.com. But, these usually have prices for only a few cards in a set. And, they are not updated regularly.

One of the best online price guides for sports cards is beckett.com. It offers price guides for baseball, football, basketball, hockey, racing, golf, and Pokémon cards. However, it does cost a small fee to use the service.

Magazines

If you don't have Internet access, your best bet is a price guide magazine. You can also take price guide magazines to card shows or stores. Like its online guides, Beckett's price guide magazines are popular among collectors.

There are several other good sports card guides available too. These include *Tuff Stuff*, *Sports Market Report*, and *Sports Collectors Digest*. If you're looking for CCG card prices, you'll find that magazines such as *Beckett Yu-Gi-Oh* or *Scrye* are your best resources.

Books

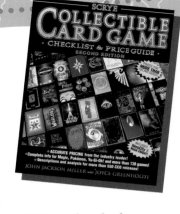

Sports card pricing companies such as Beckett and Sports Collectors Digest produce annual books that list all the card values for a particular sport. Many of these books list card prices for past years too. The 2006 edition of the *Baseball Card Price Guide* has values for cards up to 15 years old.

These books are helpful if you have a lot of older cards that you need to keep track of. But since they are updated only once a year, they are not as current as online price guides or magazines. For CCG pricing, collectors should check out *Scrye's Collectible Card Game Checklist & Price Guide*. It contains pricing on more than 150 different CCGs.

No Dough?

Do you want to check a card's value without spending money? Your local library might have a **subscription** to a card pricing magazine. Even if it doesn't, it will surely have an annual price guide you can check out or read there.

Grading a Card's Condition

You've probably noticed that price guides often list two or three prices for each card. This is because the condition of a card has a dramatic effect on its value. A card in mint condition is worth more than that same card in good condition. Being able to judge the condition of a card will help you get the best value when you are buying, selling, or trading.

Card Grades

GEM-MT 10: Gem Mint. A perfect card.

MINT 9: Mint. May have a very slight wax stain on the reverse, a minor printing imperfection, or slightly off-white borders.

NM-MT 8: Near Mint-Mint. May show the slightest fraying at one or two corners.

NM 7: Near Mint. Minor surface wear may be visible.

EX-MT 6: Excellent-Mint. May have a very light scratch or loss of original gloss. Multiple corners may have slight fraying.

EX 5: Excellent. A very minor rounding of the corners may be present. Surface wear or printing defects may be visible. There may be minor chipping on edges.

VG-EX 4: Very Good-Excellent. The card may have a light crease, and light scuffing may be visible.

VG 3: Very Good. The photo may be somewhat out of focus, and the edges may have noticeable wear. Most of the card's original gloss is gone, and the borders may be discolored.

GOOD 2: Good. The card's corners may be noticeably rounded. There may be several creases, and surface wear is starting to become obvious.

PR-FR 1: Poor to Fair. The card's corners and surface will show extreme wear, including scuffing, scratching, creasing, pitting, chipping, staining, and soiling.

Buying and Selling

A FEW LARGE RETAIL STORES SELL UNOPENED PACKS OF COLLECTIBLE CARDS. But their selection is limited, and they don't buy or sell individual cards. Fortunately, you can find a great selection of cards at game and hobby stores. The Internet also has become a important resource for collectors of all types.

Hobby Shops

BUYING

Hobby shops usually have a good selection of sports cards and CCGs. The staff usually will be knowledgeable enough to help you find what you need. Most hobby shops sell packs, individual cards, and packaged assortments of loose cards. It's nice to see the cards in person before you buy them. Some shops will write the card's grade on the casing. But always make sure to **evaluate** the card yourself.

SELLING

Hobby shops need to make a profit. So, they buy cards at a low price and sell them for more. You could probably sell a card to another collector for more than your local hobby shop would pay for it. But if you want to sell some cards quickly and easily, a hobby shop might be your best option.

Card Shows and Tournaments

BUYING

Card shows, tournaments, and conventions can be fantastic places to build your collection. When dealers and collectors gather to buy, sell, trade, and discuss cards, there are sure to be some interesting deals! Prices are generally lower than at hobby stores, depending on the size, location, and function of the show. Check your local hobby shop, a card-collecting magazine, or the Internet for upcoming shows or tournaments near you.

SELLING

Because there are so many dealers in one spot, a card show can be a good place to get a fair price for your unwanted cards. Ask a few different dealers what they would pay for your cards before you sell them.

The Internet

BUYING

The majority of the merchants found using search engines such as yahoo.com or google.com sell cards for about twice the values listed in price guides. It's not uncommon to pay more than the listed price for a card in near-mint or mint condition. But because you can't examine the card when buying online, it's important to look for graded cards. That way, you'll be certain of the quality of card you're purchasing. Be sure to check the site's return policy. If the card isn't the quality advertised, you want to be able to return it.

If you're looking for a deal, check out **auction** sites such as ebay.com, beckett.com, or etopps.com. There's more risk involved, but the prices may be better than buying from online stores. It's always a good idea to check the reputations of the sellers before bidding. If their previous buyers were dissatisfied, think twice about purchasing from them.

Finally, when buying online, check the cost of shipping. That adds to the cost of the cards you buy.

SELLING

Internet auctions are one way to get top value for your cards. You need to be familiar with the Internet auction process. And, you have to be willing to package and ship your cards. You will need an adult to help you set up an account to sell your cards.

If your cards are valuable, consider having them professionally graded. Graded cards are easier to sell because the buyer is more certain of their condition.

A graded card

Graded Cards

Graded baseball cards have been **evaluated** by a grading company. The company assigns a grade based on the condition of the card. Then, it seals the card in a plastic case. Cards in better condition are worth more money. You must pay a fee to get a sports card or a CCG card graded. Some people collect only graded cards.

Trading

WHATEVER TYPES OF CARDS YOU COLLECT, TRADING CAN BE ONE OF THE MOST ENJOYABLE WAYS TO IMPROVE YOUR COLLECTION. It's also a fun way to hang out with friends or classmates! If you have an extra copy of a card that another collector wants, you could trade it for a card that you like. Both collectors improve their collections, and everyone is happy!

But trading goes far beyond unwanted duplicates. Depending on what your collecting goals are, you can use different trading **strategies** to help you meet those goals.

Let's say you're collecting a complete set of 2005 Topps football cards. But, you're missing about 12 minor cards. And, let's say your classmate collects Peyton Manning cards. He also has all the cards you need to complete your set. Normally, you wouldn't trade a star player like Manning for lesser cards. But in this case, you might want to because you can complete your set.

If you play a CCG, you've probably already created a strategic deck. And, you probably have some leftover cards that you don't use often. You could start a second strategic deck with these cards. Keep the more powerful cards and trade the others for cards that work well with them.

Organization and Storage

Types of Storage Devices

SOFT SLEEVES. Soft sleeves are cheap, card-sized sleeves of soft plastic. They protect single cards from surface wear, but not much else.

TOP LOADERS. Top loaders are made of a harder, bendable plastic. They are slightly larger than soft sleeves. Their rigidity protects single cards from creasing and corner wear. Collectors often put a card in a soft sleeve before putting it into a top loader.

STORAGE BOXES. Storage boxes are cardboard boxes that have been specially designed to hold trading cards. They come in many sizes. Some can hold thousands of cards. And, some are made to fit cards in soft sleeves or top holders.

ALBUMS AND PAGES. These books are similar to photo albums. The clear plastic sheets hold up to nine cards each.

SCREW-DOWN CASES. Screw-down cases are two blocks of thick, unbendable plastic. You put the card between them and screw the pieces together.

Use the Right Kind of Storage

STORING COMMON CARDS

Cardboard boxes made for trading cards are great for storing lots of common cards. They have built-in dividers and can hold up to 5,000 cards per box! All the cards should stand straight up, and each row should be comfortably filled. If a row has too many cards, you may damage a card's edges when you try to remove it. If the rows are packed too loosely, some cards will fall over and get bent.

STORING FAVORITE CARDS

For cards that you show off or play with often, a card album with clear plastic sheets works great. The soft plastic helps protect the surface of the cards. And, the album's rigid binding protects their shape and edges. In addition, both the front and back of each card can be viewed easily. Albums are easy to take with you to a friend's house, a convention, or a CCG tournament. However, they are fairly expensive. If you're looking to save a few dollars, you could put your favorite cards in top-loaders instead. Keep them in a small cardboard box that's easy to carry.

Card Bookend

Do you have a row in your box that's only partially filled? You can make a temporary "bookend." Just fill the remaining space with Styrofoam or cardboard inserts. That way, your cards won't fall over and get damaged.

STORING PREMIUM CARDS

If you have cards that are worth ten dollars or more, consider displaying them in screw-down cases. Not only do cards look great in these cases, they're protected well too. However, don't transport cards in these cases. Too much movement may cause the cards to shift inside the cases.

STORING COMPLETE SETS

Most collectors prefer to store complete sets separate from the rest of their collection. A complete set of cards often comes in its own box. Since the set fits perfectly in the box, there's no reason to move it to a new box. If you've collected the set one card at a time, try to find a cardboard box that's about the same size as or a little larger than your set.

Track Your Cards Using a Computer

Many new collectors think their collection is too small to track. Nonsense! The sooner you begin, the easier it will be to track your cards as your collection grows. If you have a computer, software programs can make tracking a collection easier.

My Collections

There's a fantastic feature on beckett.com called My Collections. My Collections lets you track and find updated values for each card in your collection. You'll need an online **subscription** to beckett.com to see the values for individual cards. But if you just want to see the value of your total collection, there is no fee. All you need to do is register with the site. My Collections allows you to scan and upload images of your cards. Then you can see them online! The program also lets you track cards that you don't own but want to collect.

Using a spreadsheet

If you have spreadsheet software, such as Microsoft Excel, you can use it to track your cards. Simply enter a card's description, the set of cards it's in, and its current value. There are disadvantages to this method, however. It takes more time, and you'll have to update the prices manually.

Conclusion

Whatever types of cards you collect, remember that the point is to have fun! Whether you're trading sports cards with your classmates or going head-to-head in a CCG, collectible cards are a great way to spend time with your friends. Don't get too caught up in the monetary value of your collection. The real value of the cards is the experiences you have collecting them!

Glossary

animation – a sequence of still images intended to create the illusion of motion.

auction – a sale in which goods are sold to the highest bidder.

autograph – a person's handwritten name.

covet – to wish for greatly or with envy.

culture – the characteristics of a racial, religious, or social group.

etching – a design on a hard material with lines dug into the material's surface.

evaluate – to study something in order to determine its value or worth.

intriguing – very interesting or fascinating.

poised – ready or in position to do something.

random – having no pattern or plan.

rookie – a first-year player in a sport.

statistics – a collection of numerical data.

strategy – a plan for achieving a specific goal.

subscription – an agreement to purchase a series of items in advance.

World War II – a global conflict that ended in 1945.

Web Sites

To learn more about cool cards, visit ABDO Publishing Company on the World Wide Web at **www.abdopublishing.com.** Web sites about cool cards are featured on our Book Links page. These links are routinely monitored and updated to provide the most current information available.

Index